Disclaimer: The advice and recipes in this book are published for general interest for the reader only. This information is not intended to take the place of medical guidelines and recommendations by medical professionals. Please be advised that none of this material is intended to be construed as health care advice; it is not the Author's intent to give professional advice to the individual reader. The information should not be used in place of appropriate medical treatment and is in no way tailored to the needs of the reader's specific situation. The reader is advised that the suggestions in this book are based on the Author's own experience and do not (and cannot) replace consultation with a doctor and/or nutritionist where health matters are concerned. The Author makes no express or implied representation, warranty, or guarantee as to the completeness, accuracy, or currency of the information contained herein, or its suitability for any particular purpose, as information relevant to nutrition and medicine is constantly evolving as research develops and continues. The reader is cautioned to refrain from relying upon any of the information in this book as a substitute for consultations with qualified health professionals who are familiar with the reader's specific medical needs. Meniere's disease, as does any health related issue, requires medical supervision, and therefore, the reader should consult with the appropriate health care provider, without delay, if there are any concerns or questions about the subject. The Author's opinions expressed in this book are derived from her own personal experience and thus, the Author shall not be responsible or liable for any injury, damage or loss arising from information or suggestions in this book. Although every effort has been made to provide accurate and complete information at the date of publication, exact measurements and cooking times are dependent upon factors, including but not limited to the quality of ingredients and the varying temperatures of kitchen equipment. Therefore, the readers' commonsense as well as familiarity with personal kitchen equipment should be utilized accordingly. The Author shall take no responsibility for individual health issues or specific allergies, known or otherwise, that need specific medical supervision or any adverse reaction to any ingredient specified or any adverse reactions to the recipes contained in this book. To be sure, the recipes contained in this book are not intended to be a cure for Meniere's disease and should not be interpreted as such. The use of any information provided in this book is solely at the reader's own risk.

Ménière's Cookbook

Exquisite Gluten-Free Recipes From Around The World

Eight years. That is how long it took for me to heal myself of Ménière's disease, a chronic disorder of the inner ear. It was a journey of exploration and courage, curiosity and stamina that eventually lead to my recovery.

Whether you have Ménière's or Celiac disease, a non-celiac gluten sensitivity, a wheat allergy or just want to have a healthy diet and lifestyle, this cookbook is for you. Being diagnosed with Ménière's disease at the age of 28 and going through the ups and downs of the illness plus trying everything except for surgery, I have concluded that a healthy diet is a key factor in fighting Ménière's and many other illnesses.

Ménière's disease causes vertigo and dizziness as well as fluctuating hearing loss, ringing in the ear (tinnitus), and ear pressure. The disease is named after the French physician Prosper Ménière, who in 1861 first reported that vertigo was caused by inner ear disorders.

Through my journey with this disabling condition I discovered many triggers, most of which turned out to be particular foods and beverages I consumed. As time went by, I began making mental notes of what they were and adjusted my diet and lifestyle in order to avoid them. Now, I have finally gained control over my symptoms and want to share my secrets with you, fellow Meniere's sufferers and their loved ones.

It is my hope that this cookbook will help set you on the path towards living a healthier lifestyle and becoming symptom-free through my organic, gluten-free and anti-inflammatory recipes. You will enjoy creating these wholesome dishes that I have discovered through many trips to various countries and during my experiences living abroad.

Bon Appétit!

Contents

My Triggers

Gluten: Gluten is composed of many different proteins. There are two main groups of proteins in gluten, called the gliadins and the glutenins. Gluten is found mainly in wheat, barley and rye and a cross between wheat and rye called triticale. Gluten can be found in a large variety of foods including soups, salad dressings, processed foods, soy sauce and beer. This bad boy is the biggest of my triggers and only until after I had given up gluten was I able to stop taking my Meniere's medicine. This personal discovery is why I decided to write a gluten-free cookbook, as it is my belief that gluten strongly contributed to my getting ill in the first place.

Sodium: Table Salt is a manufactured form of sodium called sodium chloride. More than 75 percent of the sodium in the average American diet comes from table salt added to processed foods. In other words, we often don't even know we are eating it. Sodium shows up in canned soups, salad dressings and even products that don't immediately come to mind when we think of 'salty' foods, such as pasta, ketchup, bread and cereals. I now use Himalayan pink salt, which has less sodium than sea salt, but always in moderation (1 teaspoon per day) and avoid processed foods.

Caffeine: All things made with caffeine such as sodas, energy drinks and coffee products are a big NO-NO in my diet because they cause a stuffy head feeling, headaches and brain fog. I also avoid decaffeinated coffee as it still has traces of caffeine, plus the decaffeination process is performed with harmful chemicals. There is a "coffee" I buy online which is actually not made from coffee beans, but instead from figs that successfully takes away my coffee cravings and is actually pretty delicious!

Teas: I avoid black, green and Jamaica flower teas since they also make my head feel stuffy. I do drink herbal teas such as mint, chamomile or rooibos when I am craving a hot beverage. I also make my own infusions at home with fresh ginger, mint, basil and fresh fruits.

Smoking: This horrible habit clogs up my inner ear and causes me to have dizziness, vertigo and migraines. Therefore, I stay away from cigarettes, pipes, hookahs and cigars.

Aspartame: This toxic artificial sweetener has been linked to brain cancer, seizures, depression, lupus and multiple sclerosis, chronic fatigue syndrome, Parkinson's disease, Alzheimer's, mental retardation, Lymphoma, birth defects, fibromyalgia, diabetes, arthritis (including Rheumatoid) and attention deficit disorder. In an epidemiological survey, which appeared in the Journal of Applied Nutrition (Roberts 1988), 551 persons who have reported toxicity effects from aspartame ingestion were surveyed.[1] The adverse effects found cover a subset of reported acute and chronic toxicity effects from aspartame in the ear: 73 persons with tinnitus, 47 with severe intolerance to noise and 25 with marked impairment of hearing. Aspartame is everywhere you see the word light or diet. I noticed it triggered my dizziness and made me feel nauseated, especially when I chewed gum. If you are a chewer, it is time to spit that piece of poisonous gum out!

Canned Foods: Most canned foods are lined with the hormone-disrupting Bisphenol A (BPA) which is a high production volume chemical used in a variety of common consumer products. Most notably, BPA is present in polycarbonate plastics, the epoxy resin liners of aluminum cans, and thermal receipts (Ehrlich et al. 2014).[2] Canned foods also have very high sodium content, so it is better to stay clear of them. Instead of choosing canned, I go with jarred versions of Mediterranean tuna and caper berries as well as boxed coconut milk.

Drinking Alcohol:
If I am dizzy, the last thing I want is to get dizzier through ingesting alcohol. However, if I feel fine and fancy a drink, I stick to organic wine and organic gluten-free beer. I do not drink hard liquor because the majority of the time it is not organic and when mixed with any juice, it just adds a lot of sugar and sodium to the equation.

Pesticides, Herbicides, & Fungicides:
As you may have noticed, these are poisons that ironically all rhyme with the word "suicide," and why would anyone in their right mind want to ingest poison?! I buy everything organic and even wash the organic products extremely well to avoid cross-contamination. I notice that when I eat out in restaurants that are not organic, my symptoms start to return despite my ordering foods without salt.

Cured Meats:
These meats have been treated with salt and nitrate. The salt dehydrates the meat and the nitrate releases nitrous acid to achieve an attractive pink color when cooked. Cured meats include bacon, hams, salami, prosciutto and sausages. Nothing with that much sodium can be good for a person with Meniere's or anyone in general, so I avoid these at all costs.

The Cold:
The cold weather always attacks my ear and triggers my vertigo, which is one of the reasons I left New York City for sunny Rome. If you live in a cold area, make sure you cover your ears very well before going outside. I usually put on a headband and then ear muffs on top for double coverage. I also try to avoid very cold beverages and places with high air conditioning.

Dairy Products:
Beware of these, especially in the form of cheese as they are made with a lot of sodium and in most cases with table salt. I limit myself to a bit of parmigiano or pecorino (sheep cheese) for my gluten-free pasta dishes and risottos, and use feta cheese for some of my other dishes. Since it's not easy to find organic cheeses in the States, I choose those imported from Italy, Spain or Greece because treating cows, sheep and goats with hormones in the European Union is prohibited. I also buy unsalted organic butter for my tomato pasta sauce, but stay clear from everything else made from cow's milk due to dairy being a known inflammatory to the human body.

Sugar:
I believe high fructose corn syrup triggers my attacks either because the corn is genetically modified or it is full of pesticides. White sugar, since it goes through a bleaching process is toxic for the body as well. I opt for natural sweeteners like raw honey, panela (unrefined whole cane sugar) and real maple syrup (choose carefully as some are not authentic).

Soy:
Soy sauce can trigger my attacks because it has very high sodium content and has gluten! I use organic low sodium tamari sauce, which is the gluten-free version of soy sauce, but always in moderation.

Air Travel:
Flying can be a pain when you have Meniere's as the cabin pressure can make your inner ear swell up, which of course triggers vertigo and dizziness. Traveling with someone always helps, but if you are traveling solo, you can notify the crew of your condition so that they take proper care of you in case of an attack. I usually give myself a day or two to rest after a flight before making any appointments or plans.

My Helpers

Anti-Inflammatory Foods:
I use these helpers to aid me in reducing the inflammation in my body caused by years of eating gluten. They are full of vitamins, minerals and antioxidants, and some of them (coconut oil, ginger and garlic) are even antibacterial, antiviral and antifungal! All of these amazing foods are repeatedly included in my recipes:

Turmeric Root	Coconut Oil	Olive Oil
Fatty Fish &	Leafy Greens	Asparagus
Seafood	Garlic & Onions	Berries
Almonds	Dark Chocolate	Chia Seeds
Walnuts	Grapes	Broccoli
Ginger Root	Raisins	Flax Seeds
Shitake-	Chickpeas	
Mushrooms	Avocado	

Natural Diuretic Foods:
I eat these lovely helpers very often and they are all included in my cookbook. They help flush out excess sodium and toxins from my body as well as to give me the energy I need to have a productive day.

Cucumbers	Apples	Cilantro
Pineapple	Celery	Carrots
Asparagus	Garlic & Onions	Ginger
Watermelon	Cabbage	Beets
Parsley	Lemon	Berries
Tomatoes	Mango	Apple Cider-
Bananas	Herbal Teas	Vinegar
Fennel	Coconut	
Artichokes	Eggplant	

Fresh Organic Fruits and Vegetables:
I cannot put enough emphasis on how important it is to eat organic. I try to eat my fruits and veggies fresh and mostly raw so that the body can absorb the nutrients, minerals and vitamins in the best way. I make myself a power juice in the morning with fruits, veggies, seeds and coconut oil, which serves as my multivitamin ☺ (see recipe on page 17).

Coca Leaf Tea:
This tea is native to South America, particularly from the Andes mountain region. The potential benefits of coca tea may include energy, immunity boost and relief of indigestion and altitude sickness. I discovered this tea a few years back on a trip to Colombia. I found that on me, it has an effect similar to that of Betahistine, which is the medicine I was last taking for Meniere's.

Kombucha:
This ancient fermented tea-based probiotic beverage has been used as a healing tonic for at least 3,000 years. It is believed to provide healthful micronutrients and bacteria beneficial to digestion, detoxification and immunity. This delicious probiotic tea doesn't trigger my symptoms like other teas and helps me keep a healthy gut. There are other probiotic products you can buy such as sauerkraut or Korean kimchi; just remember to always choose the organic versions.

Water:
I drink a lot of water to stay hydrated and flush out the toxins and excess sodium from my body. I do, however, buy water by the gallon that comes from a mountain source and has been bottled in glass 5-gallon jugs. I avoid tap water since in most states in this country it is treated with chloride and sodium fluoride. I also avoid plastic bottled water at all costs because the majority of plastic is made with Bisphenol A (BPA) and other toxic materials.

Sleep:
As some of you may know, sleep really helps when you feel dizzy and have extreme fatigue. I often take naps in the afternoons and sometimes even in the mornings; I try not to fight them as they are big helpers. Even a 10-minute nap will make a difference in my day and give me an energy boost.

My Advice

GMOs: ("genetically modified organisms") are living organisms whose genetic material has been artificially manipulated in a laboratory through genetic engineering, or GE. This relatively new science creates unstable combinations of plant, animal, bacteria and viral genes that do not occur in nature or through traditional crossbreeding methods. Virtually, all commercial GMOs are engineered to withstand direct application of herbicide and/or to produce an insecticide. Despite biotech industry promises, none of the GMO traits currently on the market offer increased yield, drought tolerance, enhanced nutrition, or any other consumer benefit. Meanwhile, a growing body of evidence connects GMOs with health problems, environmental damage and violation of farmers' and consumers' rights.[3] The most common GMOs you will encounter are corn, soy, beets, potatoes and oils such as canola and cottonseed. Always choose organic and check for the NON-GMO project logo.

Poultry and Eggs:
I keep chicken intake to a minimum and use an average of 2 eggs per week so that I can keep my estrogen levels in check. When buying chicken and eggs, always make sure that what you are getting is antibiotic-free and doesn't have added hormones. Also make sure that the chickens have had a non-GMO diet and that they have led a good life outdoors. Stay clear of eggs and chickens that say cage-free as these are most likely jam-packed together in a warehouse; opt for free range instead.

Red Meat:
I barely ever consume red meat. Only about twice a year when I got to Colombia do I have a piece of steak and some pork, but only because I know the conditions of the farms they come from and how animals are treated there. Also, since I have found that a plant-based diet is more favorable for my Meniere's, I avoid red meat. If you absolutely cannot live without red meat, make sure you choose meat from animals that are "grass-fed" since many farms feed their cows GMO corn and soy, which is something you absolutely want to avoid. The meat should also be free of antibiotics and added hormones as well as from free-range cows.

Fish & Seafood:
Make sure what you buy is wild caught or responsibly farmed. A lot of farmed fish are fed GMO corn and soy, so read the labels carefully and ask your fish seller questions about the origin of the fish. In Europe a lot of salmon, sea bream and Mediterranean sea bass are farmed but with good practices. Avoid tilapia as in most cases is fed with GMOs.

Salt:
The easiest way I found to measure salt is to cook without it and then add it to my plate by dividing the teaspoon of Himalayan pink salt I allow myself a day between my meals. Since I avoid any processed food that might have hidden sodium, I have no reaction to that teaspoon of pink salt per day. I am, however, very careful when bathing in the sea or ocean to not swallow any salt water as this does cause a vertigo attack the following day.

Going Gluten Free:
If you aren't gluten free already, you should absolutely give a gluten free diet a chance for at least 3 months (ideally 6) to see if your symptoms improve. It actually isn't as difficult as it sounds; there are so many options for gluten-free pastas such as quinoa, brown rice, corn, lentil, etc. There are also many flours made with healthy grains and nuts such as rice, almond, coconut, chickpeas, tapioca, quinoa, etc. You can find gluten-free breads now made with these flours that you can use to supplement some of your favorites foods that you use bread for. There are also legumes, healthy whole grains, potatoes, yams, plantains, cassavas and many

other starchy foods you can eat that will not make you miss wheat. You can also get tested to see if you have a wheat allergy or have sensitivity for gluten. Ask your allergist to test for Gliadin, Deamidated Gliadin and Transglutaminese 2 IgG and I gA to see if you have antibodies to gluten, which can indicate a non-celiac gluten sensitivity. However, the best way to know is to do an elimination diet as the tests available now are not very conclusive and there are many components to wheat that could be affecting your health besides the gluten proteins.

Oils:
There are a lot of bad oils out there made with GMOs such as canola, cottonseed, soybean or corn oil. I suggest you only use cold-pressed virgin olive oil and raw coconut oil for cooking. Sesame seed, avocado and olive oil are very good for salads. Stay away from margarine or any hydrogenated oils.

Go All The Way Organic:
From your food to your laundry detergent to your cleaning supplies and toiletries; this is a way that you can avoid exposure to harmful chemicals. I understand going organic can be quite costly, but your health will thank you later. I, for example, clean my apartment with white vinegar, which is inexpensive and works very well. Also, you can grow some vegetables and herbs at home or regrow some of them from kitchen scraps such as, celery, lettuce, garlic, carrots, etc.

Dining Out:
I suggest going to organic restaurants and ordering salt-free dishes. You should bring your own pink Himalayan salt with you. If you cannot avoid going to a normal restaurant (you know, since you want to have a "normal" social life), make sure you avoid gluten at all costs and ask for dishes without salt as well as water bottled in glass.

Exercise:
For Meniere's sufferers exercise could be a good or bad thing. Any exercise that requires a lot of movement or strength can cause a vertigo attack. Tennis and jogging were some of the first sports I had to give up. Now I speed-walk, ride my bicycle by the beach and attend barre classes to stay fit and maintain a healthy weight.

Work from home:
One of the things that really has helped me cope with my Meniere's is the fact that I work from home at my own pace and schedule. Two years after I had my first symptoms of Meniere's, I decided to start my own online villa rental company. This allowed me to work whenever I had the energy, nap whenever I needed and cook for myself. I know this is easier said than done, but if you are stressed and not able to give it your all at work, it will be very difficult to heal yourself.

Think about Meniere's as an opportunity to go back to school to learn a new trade or further your education. You can study from home and/or open your own business. Perhaps begin pursuing something you have always been passionate about, but never had the chance to do. Living in New York City with an extremely busy professional/social life, I really felt I needed to slow down the pace of a lifestyle I simply could not handle anymore. I pretty much had to stop and "smell the roses" so I used my savings and first moved to Rome where I learned Italian then to Paris where I studied French while working on my villa rentals online.

Now I am publishing my first cookbook, which is one of my biggest accomplishments since cuisine has always been a big passion for me and now I get to share that passion with you! Currently, I am studying holistic nutrition from home, which I absolutely love as it will prove very beneficial for my health as well as useful for my cookbooks. Therefore, do not let Meniere's disease stop you from accomplishing your dreams. Begin by changing your lifestyle and diet and you will start to discover plenty of ways to bring your life a renewed sense of joy and personal accomplishment.

Cooking Essentials

It is important you have all or most of these essentials handy when getting into your kitchen so that you can save time and energy.

Kitchen:

Measuring Cups & Spoons
Tomato Peeler with Teeth
A very good Blender
Set of Pots and Pans
Vegetable Steamer
Set of Kitchen Knives
Food Processor

Vegetable Slicer
Lemon Squeezer
Cooking Utensils
Cutting Boards
Baking Trays
Juicer
Wok

Pantry:

Dijon Mustard (from France)
Pink Himalayan Salt
Balsamic Vinegar
Extra Virgin Olive Oil
Apple Cider Vinegar
Black and Red Pepper
Coconut Oil
Coconut Milk
Coconut Water
Raw Honey
Maple Syrup (authentic)
All Purpose Gluten-Free Flour
Panela (unrefined whole cane sugar)
Baking Soda
Cinnamon (grounded and in sticks)
Vanilla Extract

Organic Herbs:

It is a good idea to keep plants of these herbs so you have easy access to them. You can also find them fresh in the supermarket as well as dry; however, if you have a choice, always go with fresh.

Oregano
Basil
Rosemary

Mint
Cilantro (coriander)
Thyme

Organic Grains & Legumes:

Keep these beauties dry in your kitchen as you could use them anytime for many of your dishes. Make sure you give your chickpeas and black beans enough time to soak (at least 6 hours). Avoid canned legumes; if you do not have the time to cook them (1-2 hours), choose the salt-free boxed version.

Black Beans
Cannellini (white) Beans
French Lentils
Arborio (risotto) Rice
Quinoa

Chickpeas
Brown Short Grain Rice
Basmati Rice
Red Split Lentils
Brown Rice/Quinoa pasta

Organic Nuts and Seeds:

Most nuts and seeds found in supermarkets are generally roasted and oftentimes in bad oils. Also, nuts and seeds naturally contain some sodium, but commercial manufacturers often add table salt to them. Always choose organic, raw and unsalted.

Raw Pine Nuts
Raw Almonds
Raw Sesame Seeds
Raw Chia Seeds
Raw Walnuts
Raw Cashews
Raw Pumpkin Seeds

Raw Flax Seeds
Raw Cashews
Raw Sunflower Seeds
Sesame Seed Tahini
Raw Unsalted Almond-Butter

Watermelon

Level: Very easy

Serves: 1

What you need:

- 1 cup of watermelon
- 1 cup of peeled cucumber
- 1 tablespoon of lemon juice

How to make it:

Blend all ingredients for a minute and voila!

Pineapple

Level: Very easy

Serves: 1

What you need:

- 1 cup of pineapple
- 1 cup of coconut water
- 1 teaspoon of coconut oil
- 1 teaspoon of fresh mint

How to make it:

Place all ingredients in a blender and blend for one minute.

Beet

Level: Easy

Serves: 1

What you need:

- ½ cup of peeled beets
- 1 pink apple
- 1 cup of carrots
- 1 tablespoon of chopped fresh ginger
- 1 teaspoon of chopped fresh turmeric root
- 1 teaspoon of fresh lemon juice

How to make it:

Place all ingredients in your juicer and serve!

Green

Level: Very easy

Serves: 1

What you need:

- 1 green apple
- 1 small cucumber with skin
- 2 celery stalks
- ½ cup of spinach
- 1 tablespoon of parsley

How to make it:

Place all ingredients in your juicer and serve!

Power Juice

Level: Easy   **Serves:** 1

I drink this juice every morning during the week. It gives me the strength to get through the morning and fills me up all the way to lunch.

What you need:

- ½ banana
- ½ cup of pineapple
- ½ cup of cucumber
- 1/3 cup of celery
- 1/3 cup of mango
- 1/3 cup of beets
- 1 half a cup of berries of your choice

- 1 tablespoon of raw almond butter
- 1 tablespoon of fresh ginger
- 1 tablespoon of coconut oil
- 1 teaspoon of flaxseeds
- 1 teaspoon of chia seeds
- 1 teaspoon of fresh turmeric root
- 1 cup of coconut water

How to make it: Blend all ingredients together until you get a smooth consistency. Add more coconut water if they juice is too thick for your taste.

Almond Flour Pancakes

Level: Easy   **Serves:** 6 medium sized pancakes

What you need:

- 1.5 cups of blanched almond flour or meal
- 1 cup of almond milk
- 3 eggs
- 1 tablespoon of coconut oil
- 1 teaspoon of vanilla extract
- A pinch of baking soda
- 1/3 cup of blueberries
- 1/3 cup of sliced banana

How to make it:

Place all ingredients in a blender and blend until you get a smooth consistency. Grease your pan with coconut oil; then add 1/6 of the mixture and cook for 1 minute over medium heat. Place your fruit on your pancake, cook for 3 minutes and then flip with a spatula and cook until firm.

Tip: If you cannot find blanched almond flour, you can make your own by soaking your almonds for a couple of hours and then removing their skin. You can let them dry over night and then blend for a few minutes.

Chia/Flax Seed Pudding

Level: Easy   **Serves:** 2 breakfast portions or 4 dessert portions

This fantastic vegan pudding will leave you very satisfied for breakfast. You can also use it as a healthy dessert.

What you need:

- ½ cup of chia seeds
- ¼ cup of flax seeds
- 1 ½ cups of coconut milk
- Berries of your choice
- 1/3 cup mango pieces
- Raw honey to taste
- Silvered almonds

How to make it: Place the seeds and coconut milk in a bowl and stir for 5 minutes. Stir again every 2 minutes for a period of 10 minutes so that the seeds don't cluster. Then place in the refrigerator to cool down for 10-15 minutes; stir again and serve in a soup bowl with the mango and berries. Top with honey to taste and sprinkle with almonds.

Breakfast Tacos

Level: Easy   **Serves:** 2 servings of 3 tacos

What you need:

- 2 eggs
- ¼ cup of cherry tomatoes cut in half
- ¼ cup of diced bell peppers
- ¼ cup of diced mushrooms
- 6 small corn tortillas
- 1 small avocado
- Hot sauce of your choice
- Cilantro to taste
- 1/2 lime cut into wedges
- Salt and pepper to taste
- Olive oil

How to make it: In a pan, sauté the tomatoes, mushrooms and peppers for 3 minutes with a teaspoon of olive oil, then add the 2 eggs and scramble with the vegetables, salt and pepper until eggs are cooked. Then serve with warm tortillas, sliced avocado, a lime wedge, chopped cilantro and hot sauce.

Tip: Add a bit of olive oil to your served scrambled eggs for extra moisture.

Avocado Toast

Level: Easy   **Serves:** 2 slices

What you need:

- 2 slices of gluten-free bread
- 1 avocado
- 2 eggs
- 1 cup of arugula
- 2 tablespoons of olive oil
- Salt and pepper to taste

How to make it: Boil your eggs for 10 minutes. Mix the arugula, salt and pepper in a bowl and serve on a plate with your toasted bread over. Add sliced avocados and eggs on top and voila!

Blackberry Jam

Level: Easy   **Serves:** 2 pieces of toast

What you need:

- 1 cup of chopped blackberries
- 1 tablespoon of honey (or to taste)
- A pinch of ground cinnamon
- 1/3 cup of water

How to make it: Place all ingredients in a small pot and cook for 10 minutes over medium heat. Towards the end smash the blackberries so you get a more even paste. Serve on toasted gluten-free bread with raw almond butter.

Tip: You can also make the jam with other fruits like peaches as they are not too acidic, unlike strawberries and raspberries. Peal and cut the peaches in small pieces and do the same process as with the blackberries.

Avocado Dip

Level: Easy   Serves: 2

This lovely dip is a more sophisticated version of guacamole and goes very well with roasted potatoes.

What you need:

- 4 medium sized avocados
- 1 tablespoon of chopped parsley
- 1 teaspoon of chopped shallot
- 1 teaspoon of chopped jalapeno (optional)
- 1 teaspoon of fresh lemon juice
- 1 tablespoon of olive oil
- Himalayan pink salt to taste

How to make it: Add all ingredients to a blender until you get a smooth consistency. Add a bit more olive oil if the paste is too thick.

Tip: Use cilantro and lime instead of parsley and lemon for a more Mexican approach.

Eggplant Dip

Level: Easy **Serves:** 2

This delicious dip is very easy to make and makes a super healthy snack; so do not fear eggplant!

What you need:

- 2 medium size eggplants
- 1 half teaspoon of garlic
- 2 tablespoons of almond butter
- 1 half teaspoon of honey
- 1 tablespoon of fresh parsley
- 4 tablespoons of olive oil
- Salt and black pepper to taste

How to make it:

Wash the eggplants and make wholes all around them with a knife or fork. Place in oven at 350-Fahrenheit degrees and bake for about 1.5 hours or until they collapse. Take them out of the oven and leave them in a strainer to drain their acidic water for at least 4 hours. For better results, let them drain over night. Then open them up in half and scoop the pulp out with a spoon; add it to your blender and blend with the rest of the ingredients.

Tip: You can replace the almond butter with tahini if you'd like. Serve with toasted gluten-free bread or crackers.

Roasted Pepper Dip

Level: Easy   **Serves:** 2

I discovered this fantastic dip at a Greek restaurant in Manhattan and it has become one of my favorites!

What you need:

- 4 big bell peppers (any color)
- 1 Teaspoon of fresh oregano (half a teaspoon if dry)
- 2 tablespoons of olive oil
- ½ teaspoon of chopped garlic
- ½ teaspoon of apple cider vinegar
- Black pepper to taste
- Pinch of Himalayan pink salt

How to make it:
Wash and put the peppers on a baking tray and place in the oven for an hour at 350-degrees Fahrenheit or until the skins start turning brown. Take the peppers out of the oven and let them cool down. Peel and seed them, then place them in a food processor with the rest of the ingredients and mix until your roasted peppers are chopped in small pieces and ready to serve.

Tip:
Serve with toasted gluten-free bread or pita. Great for the beginning of a meal or to serve with hummus and eggplant dips as a Mediterranean platter.

Hummus

Level: Medium **Serves:** 2-3

This lovely dip makes a great afternoon snack!

What you need:

- 1 cup of dried chickpeas
- ½ cup of fresh water
- 2 tablespoons of sesame tahini
- 1 garlic glove
- 4 tablespoons of olive oil
- Salt to taste
- Paprika (optional)
- 2 tablespoons of fresh lemon juice

How to make it: Soak your chickpeas for 6 hours or over night. Then drain and place them with the garlic clove in a pot with 4 times the amount of water than chickpeas. Cook for 1.5 to 2 hours until soft. When cool, place in a blender with the fresh water, olive oil, lemon juice and tahini; then mix until smooth. If your dip is too thick, add a bit more water. Salt to taste and serve in a bowl and sprinkle with paprika.

Tip: If you want a more distinct flavored hummus, you can blend in a skinned and seeded roasted pepper or eggplant. To accompany your hummus you can cut carrot, celery, fennel, and cucumber sticks.

Asparagus au Gratin

Level: Very Easy   **Serves:** 2

What you need:

- Asparagus (a handful)
- Parmigiano cheese
- Black pepper

How to make it: Cut 2 inches off the bottoms of your asparagus. Place in a pot with water and boil for 4 minutes, then drain. Place on a baking tray and add some parmigiano shavings on top (you can shave the cheese with a potato peeler). Bake for 4 minutes at 350-degrees Fahrenheit and serve with black pepper to taste. You do not need to add salt to this dish, as the cheese is pretty salty.

Tip: Your asparagus should be a bit crunchy so if you have thin asparagus, boil them for 3 minutes and bake them for another 3. If they are thick, boil them for 5 minutes and then bake for another 5.

Roman Broccoli

Level: Easy   **Serves:** 2

I discovered this absolutely amazing dish in a restaurant in Rome and it changed my life and approach to broccoli. Every time I am fortunate enough to find it in the market, I get super excited! Romanesco is more of a fall-winter vegetable so you will start seeing it from October onwards.

What you need:

- 2 cups of chopped Romanesco broccoli
- 2 tablespoons of olive oil
- 1 garlic clove
- ½ lemon
- A pinch of pepperoncino (red pepper flakes)
- Salt to taste

How to make it: Steam the chopped Romanesco for 5 minutes. Then pan sear with a tablespoon of olive oil, the garlic clove and pepperoncino for 3 minutes (make sure you do not overcook your Romanesco; it should stay firm and crunchy for serving). You can either mince the garlic or throw it in whole for taste, and then take it out at the end. Turn the burner off and add the other tablespoon of olive oil, the juice of your half lemon and then salt to taste. Stir for a couple of seconds, then serve hot with the bit of sauce left over in the pan after mixing.

Beet Leaves

Level: Easy   Serves: 2

I discovered this amazing dish at an Italian restaurant in New York City and adapted it to my taste by adding a touch of coconut.

What you need:

- 2 cups of chopped beet leaves
- 2 tablespoons of coconut milk
- 1 tablespoon of coconut oil
- 1 tablespoon of golden raisins
- 1 teaspoon of pine nuts
- Salt and pepper to taste

How to make it: In a wok or deep pan, add the washed and chopped pieces of the beet leaves with the coconut milk, coconut oil, raisins, salt and pepper. Cook until soft and the milk is reduced to a sauce (about 10 minutes). Serve warm and top with pine nuts.

Tip: The original recipe was made with red Suisse chard, but since I eat so many beets and didn't really know what to do with the leaves, I decided to use them for this recipe. You can of course use the red Suisse chard if you don't find the beet leaves. This warm appetizer also pairs nicely with lamb, steak or duck.

Roman Artichokes

Level: Medium   **Serves:** 2

Every time I make these beauties, I travel back in time to Rome. They are called carciofi alla romana in Italian.

What you need:

- 4 baby or 2 medium sized artichokes
- 2 tablespoons of white wine (optional)
- 2 tablespoons of chopped mint
- 2 tablespoons of olive oil
- 2 garlic cloves
- 2 lemons
- Salt and pepper to taste

How to make it:
Squeeze the juice of 1 lemon into a medium size salad bowl and set aside. Remove the outer layers of your artichokes until you start to see the leaves turn yellow. Discard the leaves and soak your artichokes in the lemon water. One by one remove each artichoke from the water and cut the very top green part of it off, as it is not edible. Next, you want to skin the stem and cut off any green pieces left around the base of your artichoke (heart).

At this point they should look more or less like a lollipop (see photo). You will then place your cleaned artichokes in a pot with enough water to cover them, along with the olive oil, the juice of the other lemon, the 2 peeled garlic cloves, the wine and chopped mint. Add a bit of salt and pepper to taste. Cover your pot with aluminum foil and cook the artichokes for at least 45 minutes. Check them by poking them in the heart with a fork so see if they are soft enough (they should be very soft). It might take up to 2 hours to cook depending on the size of the artichokes. Serve with a bit of the water you cooked them in. You can add a bit more olive oil and lemon when you serve them.

Tip: Try to find baby artichokes as they only take 45min to cook and the choke is not spiky yet. The bigger artichokes have a spikier center that takes a very long time to cook (approx. 2 hours). You can see the video on how to peel an artichoke in my youtube channel (Cooking with Adriana Londono).

Spaghetti Squash

Level: Medium   **Serves:** 2-3

You can find this lovely squash in the fall and winter months.

What you need:

- 1 small spaghetti squash
- 4 cups of peeled and chopped tomatoes
- 2 garlic cloves (whole)
- 2 tablespoons of butter
- 4 tablespoons of olive oil
- 1 teaspoon of honey or maple syrup
- ¼ teaspoon of red pepper flakes (optional)
- Salt to taste
- 2 tablespoons of chopped basil
- Pecorino or parmigiano cheese (optional)

How to make it:
In a big pot, place your spaghetti squash and cook for at least an hour until soft. You can poke it with a fork to make sure it is cooked all the way. Take it out of the pot and let it cool for a few minutes. While the squash is cooking, place your peeled tomatoes in a wok and start cooking at medium heat. After 30 minutes of cooking, you can add the butter and honey and stir (this helps take away the acidity of the tomatoes). Let your sauce reduce for another 20-30 minutes in low heat until you get a pasty consistency. Now you can turn off the heat and add the pepper flakes and salt to taste. Cut your spaghetti squash in half, take the seeds out with a spoon and throw them away. With a fork remove the pulp from the squash (which will come out in strings), then add it to the wok with the tomato sauce. Add your olive oil and mix together until the sauce is evenly distributed with the squash strings (just like real spaghetti). Garnish with the fresh basil and grated pecorino; then serve!

Kale & Feta Pie

Level: Easy **Serves:** 2

In my attempt to recreate something similar to the Greek spanakopita, I came up with this lovely pie.

What you need:

- 2 cups of chopped kale
- ½ cup of crumbled sheep feta cheese
- ¼ cup of grated parmigiano cheese
- 2 tablespoons of all purpose gluten-free flour
- 1 tablespoon of olive oil
- Black pepper to taste
- 2 eggs
- 1 garlic clove

How to make it:
In a large pan or wok, sauté the kale for a couple of minutes with the garlic clove. Remove the clove and then mix the sautéed kale with the rest of the ingredients except for the parmigiano. Place in a small non-stick baking pan, then sprinkle with parmigiano and bake for 10 minutes at a 350-degrees Fahrenheit.

Tip: You can also do this dish with spinach, or even better with spinach and kale☺.

Rosemary Potatoes

Level: Easy   **Serves:** 2

What you need:

- 2 cups of diced potatoes (heirloom preferable)
- 2 garlic cloves
- 2 tablespoons of olive oil
- A bunch of fresh rosemary
- Salt and black pepper to taste

How to make it:
On a baking tray, place the diced potatoes, olive oil, salt, pepper, peeled garlic cloves and rosemary. Mix everything with your hands until every potato piece is oiled. Bake at 350-degrees Fahrenheit for at least 20-30 minutes until soft.

Tip: If you like your potatoes very crunchy bake at 400 degrees to get that extra crunch. Serve with avocado dip (see recipe on page 29) or as a side dish for fish, chicken or steak.

Zucchini Salad

Level: Easy   **Serves:** 2

I discovered this fantastic salad while visiting a friend in Kenya. Light and refreshing; just perfect for a summer day.

What you need:

- 2 long and green zucchinis with skin
- 2 tablespoons of fresh squeezed lime juice
- 2 tablespoons olive oil
- Salt and black pepper to taste

How to make it:
Slice the zucchinis thinly with a vegetable slicer, then place in a bowl and add the lime juice. Salt to taste and place the bowl in the refrigerator for an hour or so. When the time is up, the bowl will be filled with water from the zucchinis. Drain a bit of the water and add the olive oil and pepper, then serve!

Tip: You can add white mushrooms and go through the same process as with the zucchinis and serve as a carpaccio. This goes lovely with hummus and Mediterranean platters.

Ratatouille

Level: Easy   **Serves:** 2

I couldn't get enough ratatouille when I was living in France a few years back. I loved it as a side for white fish and it is good anytime of year.

What you need:

- ½ cup of diced sweet bell peppers
- ¼ cup of diced onions of any color or shallots
- ½ cup of diced tomatoes
- ½ cup diced eggplant
- 2 tablespoons of olive oil,
- 1 teaspoon of apple cider vinegar
- Salt and pepper to taste

How to make it: Place all ingredients into a deep pan or wok with a 1/2 cup of water. Cover pan and cook over medium heat for 10 minutes and then uncover and simmer for another 15-20 until the vegetables are all cooked. You will know your ratatouille is done when the eggplant is soft. Add additional water if needed. The final result should look like the photo.

Tip: If you have leftover ratatouille, you can refrigerate or freeze it and then add it to gluten-free pasta as a sauce with fresh basil and parmigiano or pecorino cheese. Ratatouille pasta is actually delish!

Fennel Salad

Level: Easy   **Serves:** 2

What you need:

- 2 medium sized fennels
- ½ a lemon (squeezed)
- 2 tablespoons of olive oil
- Salt and black pepper to taste

How to make it: Slice the fennel very thinly with a vegetable slicer; if you do not have one, do it with a knife and slice it as thin as possible. In a bowl mix the sliced fennel, the lemon juice, olive oil, salt and pepper to taste and serve.

Tip: This wonderful salad makes for a great side dish to a grilled salmon or steak. It is also nice when served in a Mediterranean platter with hummus.

Green Salad

Level: Easy   Serves: 2

This lovely green salad is the perfect companion to the eggplant parmigiana (see recipe on page 115).

What you need:

- 2 cups of fresh arugula or greens of your choice or both
- 2 tablespoons of olive oil
- 1 tablespoon of Dijon mustard
- 1 teaspoon of balsamic vinegar
- Salt and pepper to taste

How to make it: In a small bowl whisk the oil, vinegar and Dijon mustard until you get a creamy texture. Taste and add salt and pepper to suit your palette. Beware that mustard already has salt. Mix greens with creamy balsamic dressing and voila!

Tip: If you are a meat lover, you can grill a peace of steak and slice it over this wonderful green salad. Serve with cherry tomatoes and parmigiano shavings.

Shitake Quinotto

Level: Easy   Serves: 2

This very healthy dish goes lovely with grilled fish or chicken.

What you need:

- 1 cup white quinoa
- 1 cup of chopped shitake mushrooms
- 3 tablespoons of pecorino or parmigiano cheese (optional)
- 1 garlic clove
- 1 tablespoon of chopped parsley
- 2 tablespoons of olive oil
- Black pepper to taste

How to make it: In a small pot heat the quinoa and garlic clove in 2 cups of water. Cook for about 10 minutes over medium heat; then add the shitake mushrooms and chopped parsley and cook for another 10 minutes. Add olive oil, pepper and cheese and mix; then serve!

Tip: If you don't want to eat the garlic, just take it out; I usually just use it for taste. If you are a garlic lover, you can mix it in with your quinotto.

Cauliflower Purée

Level: Easy   **Serves:** 2

This amazing purée goes very well with fish or chicken and tastes like heaven.

What you need:

- 2 cups of chopped cauliflower
- 1 garlic clove
- 2 tablespoons of olive oil
- Salt and pepper to taste

How to make it: Steam your cauliflower with the garlic clove for about 10 minutes or until soft; then place in a mixer with or without the garlic (up to you/your choice), the olive oil, salt and pepper. Mix for a minute and serve!

Gazpacho

Level: Easy   **Serves:** 2-3

This is my favorite summer soup and you won't believe how easy it is to make. I usually make about a liter and keep it handy in the fridge. Every time I have a sip, I feel transported to the Spanish island of Ibiza.

What you need:

- 1 cup of peeled and seeded bell peppers
- 1 cup of peeled and seeded tomatoes (heirloom preferably)
- 1 cup of peeled and seeded cucumbers
- ¼ cup of yellow onion
- 1 teaspoon of minced garlic
- 2 tablespoons of fresh lemon juice
- 1 teaspoon of apple cider vinegar
- 3 tablespoons of olive oil
- Salt and pepper to taste

How to make it: Blend all the ingredients well until you get a very liquid and even consistency. You can add extra olive oil or lemon, and garlic or onion to taste. Put in a pitcher and refrigerate for at least 3 hours, then serve!

Tip: You can make your gazpacho spicy by throwing a piece of chili to the blender. Garnish with chopped avocado and cilantro in the center and decorate with olive oil.

Chilled Avocado Soup

Level: Easy   **Serves:** 2

I first tried this soup in Villa del Mar, which is one of the villas I rent in the Colombian Caribbean. I was totally hooked on it, especially since they make their own coconut milk there!

What you need:

- 1 cup of avocado pulp
- 1 cup of coconut milk
- 1/2 cup of coconut water
- 1 teaspoon of jalapeño (optional)
- 1 teaspoon of cilantro
- Salt and pepper to taste

How to make it: Add all ingredients in a blender and mix until you get an even and smooth consistency. Place in the refrigerator to chill for 45 minutes and serve!

Minestrone

Level: Medium   **Serves:** 2-3

This amazing Italian soup is so hearty and flavorful that you wouldn't even think it doesn't need broth.

What you need:

- ½ cup of chopped and peeled carrots
- ½ cup of chopped celery
- ½ cup of chopped Swiss chard
- ½ cup of chopped and peeled zucchini
- ½ cup of chopped cauliflower
- 1/4 cup of minced and skinned onions
- 2 tablespoons of olive oil
- Salt and black pepper to taste
- Parmigiano cheese (optional)

How to make it:
In a pot, add all of the ingredients (except for the oil) with 3 cups of water and cook for 30 minutes. Add the olive oil to the soup after you have turned off your stove. Serve and garnish with grated parmigiano.

Split Lentil Soup

Level: Easy   Serves: 2

I discovered this soup in a road trip in Turkey and fell head over heels in love with it.

What you need:

- ½ cup red split lentils
- ½ cup of chopped carrots
- ½ cup of chopped celery
- ½ cup of skinned and chopped tomatoes
- ¼ cup of minced onion or shallot
- 1 garlic clove to taste
- 3 cups of water
- 3 tablespoons of olive oil
- 1 tablespoon of chopped oregano (1teaspoon if dry)
- ½ teaspoon of paprika
- 1/3 teaspoon of pepperoncino (red pepper flakes)
- 1 lemon

How to make it: Except for the olive oil and salt (which you will add when serving), add all ingredients in a pot and cook for 30 minutes at medium heat. Serve and now garnish with olive oil, salt and a lemon wedge.

Cannellini Bean Soup

Level: Easy   **Serves:** 2

I used to have this soup often for lunch while living in Rome. Romans love putting grated cheese on it but it is also very nice without.

What you need:

- ½ cup of cannellini (white) beans
- 1 cup of chopped Swiss chard
- ¼ cup of rosemary leaves
- 1 tablespoon of minced onion or shallot
- 2 tablespoons of olive oil
- Salt and black pepper to taste
- Parmigiano cheese (optional)

How to make it: Soak the beans for at least 2 hours then rinse and place in a pot. Add 2 cups of water with the Swiss chard, rosemary, onion and salt and pepper to taste. Cook for 1 hour or until your beans are cooked all the way, then add the olive oil and serve with grated parmigiano.

Tip: You can use pecorino cheese as well.

Zucchini Mint Velouté

Level: Easy   **Serves:** 2

What you need:

- 3 cups of chopped and peeled zucchini
- 1 garlic clove (whole)
- 2 tablespoons of olive oil
- 1 tablespoon of chopped mint
- Salt and black pepper to taste

How to make it: In a pot with water, place sliced pieces of zucchini with a garlic clove and cook for about 10 minutes until very soft. Then take out the pieces of zucchini and put them a blender with a little bit of the water you cooked them in, the garlic clove (optional), the mint, olive oil, salt and pepper to taste. Blend until you get a creamy, smooth consistency.

Tip: You can also make this very simple creamy soup with asparagus, just do the same procedure, but without the mint. Both soups are also nice chilled.

Artichoke Lemon Velouté

Level: Medium **Serves:** 2

This amazing velouté is delicious and despite it not having cream, tastes very creamy. I picked up this recipe at an Italian restaurant in New York City, near my office in the Upper East Side. Peeling the artichokes may take a little time, but it will all be so worth it!

What you need:

- 2 big artichokes or 4 medium sized
- 1 lemon
- 1 garlic
- 2 tablespoons of olive oil
- Salt and black pepper to taste

How to make it:
While you are peeling and cutting the artichokes, make sure that you rub half of the lemon on them so that they do not turn black. Take the leaves of the artichoke off until you see the heart and the leaves begin to turn to yellow. Cut off the stem as well as the top part of the leaves that are still green. Make sure you remove all green parts of the artichoke until the heart is completely yellow. Cut it in half and clean the furry and purple center part (choke) out with a knife until you have a shell. Then place what's left of the artichoke heart in a pot with water, the garlic clove, the juice of a half a lemon and cook for about 15 minutes until soft. Next, take out the pieces of artichoke with a bit of the water you cooked them in and put them a blender with the olive oil, salt and pepper to taste. Blend until you get a creamy, smooth consistency; add lemon to taste.

Tip: If you are not that into the citrusy taste of lemon, skip it.

Carrot Ginger Velouté

Level: Easy   Serves: 2

A friend from India taught me the recipe for this spicy soup; it is delicious and super healthy.

What you need:

- 2 cups of peeled and cut carrots
- 1 teaspoon of peeled and cut ginger
- 1 tablespoon of chopped onion or shallot
- 2 tablespoons of olive oil
- Salt and black pepper to taste

How to make it: In a pot with water, place peeled pieces of carrot, onion and ginger, and cook until very soft. Then take out the pieces of carrots and onions and put them a blender with the olive oil and a bit of the water they were cooked in. Blend until you get a creamy, smooth consistency. Add salt and pepper to taste.

Tip: Serve in a bowl and decorate with slices of ginger. You can replace the onion for garlic if you prefer a more garlicky taste.

Mushroom & Cauliflower Velouté

Level: Easy   **Serves:** 2

What you need:

- 1 cup of chopped mushrooms (white, porcini or Portobello)
- 1 cup of chopped cauliflower
- 1 garlic clove
- 1 teaspoon of chopped parsley
- 2 tablespoons of olive oil
- Salt and black pepper to taste

How to make it: In a pot with water cook the mushrooms, cauliflower and garlic clove for about 10 minutes, until very soft. Next, take out the pieces of cauliflower and mushrooms and put them a blender with a little bit of the water you cooked them in, the garlic clove (optional to taste), the parsley, olive oil, salt and pepper to taste. Blend until you get a creamy, smooth consistency.

Green Curry Soup

Level: Easy   Serves: 2

I discovered this amazing soup while on my honeymoon in Thailand.

What you need:

- 2 cups of coconut milk
- 1 cup of chopped shitake mushrooms
- 1 cup of chopped bok choy
- 2 tablespoons of green curry paste
- 2 tablespoons of chopped lemon grass or 1 tablespoon of lemongrass paste
- 1 tablespoon of chopped basil
- 1 tablespoon of coconut oil
- 1 lime
- Salt to taste

How to make it: Add all ingredients to a pot except for the lime and cook for 20 minutes. Serve with basmati rice and a lime wedge.

To make the rice: Add one cup of basmati rice to a pot with 2 cups of water, a tablespoon of coconut oil and salt to taste. Cook for 20 minutes in medium heat until the water has evaporated.

Tip: You can add a fillet of cod, halibut or Chilean sea bass to this fantastic soup; just do so 7 minutes before the soup will be done.

Greek Salad

Level: Easy   **Serves:** 2

Every time I make this fantastic salad, I get transported to the island of Mykonos with its windmills and picturesque church tops. I hope it takes you to Greece too!

What you need:
- 2 cups of your choice of greens (I usually use baby kale and spinach)
- A half of bell pepper cut in Juliennes
- 1/2 cup of chopped cucumbers
- ½ cup cherry or baby heirloom tomatoes
- Caper berries or olives (optional)
- ½ cup of sheep feta cheese

For the dressing:
- 3 tablespoons of olive oil
- Juice of half a lemon
- 1 teaspoon of chopped oregano (if dry, ½ teaspoon)
- 1 teaspoon of apple cider vinegar
- Salt and black pepper to taste

How to make it: In a small bowl whisk together the dressing ingredients until it has a creamy texture. If you want to not exceed your sodium limit, do not use salt as the cheese and olives/caper berries are salty. Mix the dressing with the vegetables. Serve on a plate topped with feta cheese and sprinkle with a pinch of oregano.

Tip: If you'd like, you can also add raw onion to the salad. Throw some sliced jalapeños if you want to make it spicy.

Mexican Salad

Level: Medium   **Serves:** 2

As a dish for lunch, this wonderful salad will leave you very satisfied and completely guilt free. You will need some time to prepare it and anticipate the soaking of the cashews and beans (at least 6 hours), and a good 45 minutes to cook the brown short-grain rice and quinoa. I discovered a similar dish in a vegan restaurant in Venice, California and adapted it to my taste.

What you need:

- 1 cup of black beans soaked (6hrs)
- 1/2 cup of short-grain brown rice
- 1 cup of raw cashews (soaked 4hrs)
- ½ cup of quinoa
- 2 cups of chopped romaine lettuce
- Half of a bell pepper cut in juliennes
- ½ cup of cherry or baby heirloom tomatoes
- ½ cup chopped tomatoes
- 1 tablespoon of sunflower seeds
- 1 tablespoon of cilantro
- Spicy sauce of your choice
- 1 tablespoon of chopped onion
- 1 avocado
- Salt to taste
- 1 lime

How to make it:

Cashew sour cream: Drain your soaked cashews and put in a blender with a bit of fresh water, the juice of half a lemon and salt. Blend until completely smooth.

The salad: Cook your soaked beans with the ½ cup of chopped tomatoes, the tablespoon of chopped onion and 4 times the amount of water for an hour or until the beans are soft. At the same time cook your rice in a pot with three times the amount of water for 45 minutes; add the quinoa to the pot for the last 20 minutes. Place the chopped romaine lettuce in 2 wide bowls with your rice/quinoa and beans. Top with cherry tomatoes, sliced avocado, sliced sweet peppers, cilantro, pumpkin seeds, cashew sour cream and your choice of hot sauce and enjoy!

Artichoke Salad

Level: Medium **Serves:** 2

This fantastic Italian salad is absolutely delicious and does very well as an appetizer or a main salad when adding prawns or shrimp.

What you need:

- 1 big or 2 medium sized artichokes
- 2 cups of arugula
- Parmigiano cheese (wedge)
- 3 tablespoons of olive oil
- Salt and pepper to taste
- 1 lemon

How to make it: (While you are peeling and cutting the artichokes, make sure that you rub half of the lemon on them so they do not turn black). Take the leaves of the artichoke off until you start seeing the leaves turn to yellow and then finally you see the heart. Then cut off the stem and the top part of the leaves that are still green. Make sure you remove all green parts of the artichoke until the heart is completely yellow. Cut it in half and then clean out the furry, purple center part (choke) with a knife until you have shell, then cut into slices and place into a pan with a bit of olive oil and sear for a couple of minutes.

In a bowl, mix the arugula, seared artichoke slices, shavings of parmigiano with olive oil, salt and pepper to taste, and the juice from the other lemon half, then serve.

Tip: Take this salad to a whole new level by adding sautéed prawns. Don't use cheese in this case as parmigiano and seafood don't really go together.

Lentil Salad

Level: Easy   **Serves:** 2-3

This lovely vegan salad is one of my latest creations. I am such a big fan of beets and fennel that I decided to mix them with French lentils to create this delicious summery salad.

What you need:

- 2 cups of greens of your choice
- ½ cup of French lentils
- ½ cup of sliced beets
- ½ cup of sliced fennel
- ½ cup of sliced carrots
- 3 tablespoons of olive oil
- 1 teaspoon of apple cider vinegar
- 1 tablespoon of Dijon mustard

How to make it:

Dressing: In a soup bowl mix the mustard, olive oil, vinegar, salt and pepper to taste. Whisk with a fork until creamy and leave aside.

Salad: Cook the lentils in a pot with water, a garlic clove and a bit of salt for 25-30 minutes. Taste them to make sure they are a bit firm as you do not want to overcook them. Drain the lentils and mix them up with the greens, fennel, carrots, beets and the dressing and serve!

Tip: You can add grilled salmon to this salad if you'd like.

Kale Caesar Salad

Level: Easy **Serves:** 2

This fantastic adaptation of the famous salad brings you to a whole new level of health via the super food kale and wholesome seeds.

What you need:

- 2 cups of Kale
- Gluten-free bread (optional)
- 1 tablespoon of sunflower seeds
- 2 egg yolks
- 1 teaspoon of anchovy paste (optional)

- ½ cup of parmigiano cheese
- 1/3 tablespoon of garlic
- 4 tablespoons of olive oil
- The juice of a half lemon
- Black pepper to taste

How to make it:

Dressing: In a blender, mix the egg yolks, parmigiano, garlic, olive oil and lemon juice. If too watery, add more cheese; taste it and see if you want to add more lemon or anchovies. The dressing should look thick and creamy. If you love garlic, then add more to your taste. The dressing doesn't need salt as the cheese and anchovies are already salty. This dressing can last up to a week in fridge.

Croutons: Cut bread in cubes, place on a baking tray with salt, pepper, and olive oil, then bake until crunchy (usually 10 minutes).

Salad: Mix dressing with chopped kale and serve with homemade croutons; sprinkle with sunflower seeds.

Tip: You can add grilled shrimp or organic chicken breast to this delicious salad.

Chickpea Salad

Level: Easy   Serves: 2

This Middle Eastern salad makes a lovely and filing lunch.

What you need:

- ½ cup of dry chickpeas
- ½ cup of chopped celery
- 1 avocado (cut to a desired size)
- 2 cups of arugula
- Juice of a half lemon
- 3 tablespoons of olive oil
- 1 teaspoon of apple cider vinegar
- Salt and black pepper to taste

How to make it: Soak the chickpeas for at least 6 hours, then drain and rise. Place in a steamer and cook for 1-1.5 hours until they are cooked enough for your taste; I like them crunchy so I only cook them for an hour. Mix with the rest of the ingredients and serve.

Tip: If you do not have time to cook the chickpeas, you can get the organic boxed version from a supermarket. Do not buy canned chickpeas. You can add jarred tuna to this salad; just make sure you use little salt as the tuna is salty.

Seafood Salad

Level: Easy   **Serves:** 2

When eaten for lunch, this delicious summery salad will leave you very satisfied.

What you need:

- 2 cups of arugula
- 1 cup of peeled and chopped potatoes
- 1 cup of peeled raw shrimp
- 1 cup of calamari (cut in rings)
- 1 cup of cherry tomatoes
- 1 tablespoon of sliced shallots
- 3 tablespoons of olive oil
- 1 tablespoon of fresh lemon juice
- Salt and pepper to taste

How to make it: Depending on the size you choose to cut the potatoes, steam them for 10-15 minutes (you can check them with a fork after 10 minutes). In the meantime add the calamari and shrimp to a pan or wok with one tablespoon of olive oil and sauté for 10 minutes. Then add the potatoes and seafood to a bowl with the rest of the ingredients and serve.

Tip: You can either serve the salad hot or cold. It's fantastic either way!

Zucchini Farfalle

Level: Easy   Serves: 2

This amazing pasta dish will leave you drooling. I discovered it when I was living in Rome and it has then become one of my signature dishes.

What you need:

- 1 cup of peeled and cut zucchini
- 2 cups of rice or quinoa pasta (dry)
- 1 tablespoon of fresh mint
- 1 egg yolk
- 1 garlic clove
- ½ cup of pecorino cheese (in chunks)
- 2 tablespoons of olive oil
- Pepper to taste

How to make it: Boil and steam the peeled zucchini with the garlic clove for 10 minutes, drain and place in a blender while still hot (you can add the whole garlic clove or just a little bit, depending how much you like garlic); then add the egg yolk, pecorino cheese, olive oil, mint and pepper. Mix until you get a creamy consistency (add more cheese if necessary) and add to your cooked pasta (follow you pasta cooking instructions); mix and serve. Decorate with mint leaves.

Rigatoni Alla Norma

Level: Easy   **Serves:** 2

This fantastic eggplant pasta is so delicious, satisfying and guilt-free!

What you need:
- 2 cups of rice rigatoni or penne pasta (dry)
- 2 cups of peeled and chopped tomatoes (in chunks)
- 1 cup of diced eggplant with skin
- 1/3 cup of ricotta salata cheese
- 3 tablespoons of olive oil
- 2 tablespoons of chopped basil
- 1 tablespoon of butter
- A pinch of red pepper flakes (optional)
- 1 garlic clove

How to make it:
In a wok, add the tomatoes, eggplant, garlic clove and butter and cook at medium-low heat for 30 minutes (the sauce will get watery and then start to reduce). Remove from heat and add the olive oil and red pepper. Cook your pasta following the instructions on its package and then mix with your sauce. Serve with crumbled ricotta salata and sprinkle with chopped basil. (This dish does not need salt as the ricotta is salty).

Tip:
Save a bit of the water you cooked the pasta in and use it for your sauce if it gets dry when mixing with the pasta. You can find ricotta salata in most supermarkets or cheese shops. It comes in a hard form and it is different from normal ricotta, which is very soft.

Lobster Spaghetti

Level: Easy   **Serves:** 2

What you need:

- 2 servings of brown rice spaghetti (check package for serving size)
- 1 cup of peeled and chopped tomatoes
- 1 cup of cherry tomatoes cut in half
- 1 cup of cooked lobster meat cut in chunks
- 3 tablespoons of olive oil
- 1 garlic clove
- 1 tablespoon of chopped basil
- A pinch of red pepper flakes or fresh chili (optional)
- Salt to taste

How to make it: In a wok or deep pan, add the chunks of peeled tomatoes and cook for 15 minutes at medium heat with the garlic clove. (In a separate pot cook your spaghetti following the packaging instructions). Add to your wok, the cherry tomatoes and lobster chunks for another 5 minutes. Add olive oil to your sauce, salt and red pepper to taste. Then mix your pasta with your sauce and serve with sprinkled chopped parsley.

Tip: If you don't want to eat the garlic whole, just take it out; I usually just use it for taste. Save a bit of the water you cooked the pasta in and use it for your sauce if it gets dry when mixing with the pasta. Italians are very against putting cheese on seafood or fish pasta; if you must, use pecorino instead of parmigiano as it goes much better.

Spaghetti Primavera

Level: Easy   Serves: 2

This lovely and light pasta is perfect for a summer lunch or dinner. I discovered it at an Italian restaurant in New York and ordered it quite often for lunch.

What you need:

- 2 servings of brown rice spaghetti (check package for serving size)
- ½ cup of chopped broccoli
- ½ cup of peeled and chopped zucchini
- ½ cup of green peas
- 1 garlic clove
- 3 tablespoons of olive oil
- Parmigiano to taste
- Salt and black pepper to taste

How to make it: Steam the broccoli, zucchini, peas and garlic clove for about 10 minutes (make sure you conserve the crunchiness of the vegetables). Cook your pasta following the instructions on its package then mix with vegetables, olive oil, salt and pepper. Serve with grated parmigiano.

Tip: If you don't want to eat the garlic whole, just take it out; I usually just use it for taste. Save a bit of the water you cooked the pasta in and use it for your sauce if it gets dry when mixing with the pasta.

Butternut Squash Risotto

Level: Medium   **Serves:** 2-3

This fantastic risotto makes an excellent companion to a meat or poultry dish. It has a twist to it because instead of using parmigiano, I use pecorino cheese.

What you need:

- 1.5 cup of Arborio white rice
- 1 cup of grated pecorino cheese
- 1 cup of chopped butternut squash
- 1/3 cup of white wine or champagne (optional)
- 3 cups of vegetable broth
- 2 tablespoons of olive oil
- 2 tablespoons fresh thyme
- 1 tablespoon of chopped shallot
- Pepper to taste

How to make it:

Broth: Follow instructions of minestrone soup to create a vegetable broth (page 67). You can use less vegetables and more water to create your broth. If you do not have all the vegetables for the broth handy, use whatever vegetables you have at home.

Butternut squash puree: In a pot, cook your squash in water for 15-20 minutes until soft. Drain and blend until you get a smooth, creamy consistency.

The risotto: In a medium deep pot, place the tablespoon of chopped shallot with two tablespoons of olive oil. Sauté the shallots until golden and then add a cup of vegetable broth. While the broth is boiling, add the Arborio rice and the white wine or champagne, the butternut squash puree and stir with a big wooden spoon. Continue to stir and add some grated pecorino, ground black pepper and thyme. As you stir and the rice starts to dry up; add more broth and continue stirring. Add more cheese until the risotto is creamy and taste it to make sure the rice is cooked al dente (the whole process shouldn't exceed 20 minutes). Serve topped with fresh thyme and some olive oil and voila!

Tip: If you do not like the strong taste of pecorino cheese, you can also do your risotto with parmigiano and it would be just as nice. I do not add salt to this dish as the cheese is already salty.

Brown Rice Risotto

Level: Medium   **Serves:** 2-3

This is such a hearty and healthy risotto that will leave you very satisfied for either lunch or dinner.

What you need:

- 1.5 cups of brown short-grained rice
- 1 cup of grated pecorino cheese
- 1/3 cup of white wine (optional)
- 4 cups of vegetable broth
- ½ cup of chopped asparagus
- ½ cup of chopped shitake mushrooms
- 1 tablespoon of chopped shallot
- 2 tablespoons of chopped parsley
- 2 tablespoons of olive oil
- Black pepper to taste

How to make it:

Broth: Follow my minestrone soup instructions to create a vegetable broth (page 67). You can use less vegetables and more water to create your broth. If you do not have all the vegetables for the broth handy, use whatever vegetables you have at home.

Risotto: In a medium sized pot, sauté the chopped shallot with the olive oil until golden; then add the rice and 2 cups of broth. Let the rice cook alone for about 25 minutes (this rice takes a good 40-45 minutes to be al dente). After 25 minutes, add a bit of grated cheese, the wine and stir always adding a bit of broth so that the rice doesn't dry up. Add the chopped asparagus, shitake mushrooms and parsley and keep stirring. Add more cheese if needed until you get a creamy consistency. Taste the rice and make sure it is cooked enough for your taste. Add pepper and more broth if needed and keep stirring. Your rice should be creamy at this point. Serve and top with a bit of olive oil and uncooked chopped parsley!

Tip: If you do not like the strong taste of pecorino cheese, you can also do it with some parmigiano and it would be as nice. I do not add salt to this dish as the cheese is already salty.

Avocado Risotto

Level: Easy   Serves: 2

This magnificent dish is so lovely and refreshing, it's perfect for a summer lunch or dinner. I saw this beauty on a menu in a restaurant in Madrid and ordered it out of curiosity. I never would have thought to put avocados in a risotto but you can and it's absolutely amazing!

What you need:

- 1.5 cups of Arborio rice
- 3 cups of vegetable broth
- 1 cup of avocado puree (do it with a blender)
- 1 tablespoon of minced shallots
- 1 cup of grated parmigiano cheese
- 1/3 cup of glass of white wine (optional)
- 1 tablespoon of chopped cilantro
- Pepper to taste

How to make it:

Broth: Follow instructions of minestrone soup to create a vegetable broth (page 67). You can use less vegetables and more water to create your broth. If you do not have all the vegetables for the broth handy, use whatever vegetables you have at home.

Risotto: In a medium sized pot, place the minced shallot with two tablespoons of olive oil. Sauté until golden and then add a cup of vegetable broth. While the broth is boiling, add the Arborio rice and white wine. Stir adding more broth so that the rice never dries up. Add the grated parmigiano and cilantro and keep on stirring until the rice is al dente and creamy enough (this should take 15-20 minutes), then add the avocado puree and chopped cilantro. Start by adding a little grated cheese until you get that creamy consistency. Serve topped with some cilantro for decoration.

Tip: Make sure you add the pureed avocados towards the end so that they do not cook too much and stay fresh. Also, when you make the avocado puree, make sure that the puree is very smooth; use a very good blender, not a chopper. I do not add salt to this dish as the cheese is already salty.

Paella Marinera

Level: Medium   **Serves:** 3-4

This Spanish beauty is absolutely delicious and not as hard to make as it looks.

What you need:

- 1.5 cups of Arborio or paella rice
- 4 cups of broth (see instructions below)
- ½ cup of chopped tomatoes
- ½ cup of sweet peas
- ½ cup of chopped bell peppers
- 1 tablespoon of chopped onion
- 1 teaspoon of chopped garlic
- 1 cup of calamari cut in rings
- 1 cup of peeled shrimp
- ½ cup of diced scallops
- 1 cup of mussels
- 1 cup of clams
- ½ cup of white wine (optional)
- 1 tablespoon of paprika
- 4 tablespoons of olive oil
- 1 teaspoon of saffron
- Salt to taste
- 1 tablespoon of chopped parsley
- Lemons

How to make it:

In a pot, boil your mussels and clams with a garlic clove and 5 cups of water and for 10 minutes. Next, strain your clams and mussels and keep the water as your broth.

In another deep pan or pot, add the chopped onions, garlic, tomatoes and peppers with a tablespoon of olive oil and sauté for a minute. Then add the broth, wine, rice, paprika and saffron and cook for 10 minutes. Now, add your seafood, peas and a bit of salt and cook for another 10 to 15 minutes and until the broth has dried up. Finally, add the rest of the olive oil, serve with lemon wedges and sprinkle with fresh chopped parsley.

Tip: Use the seafood you have handy. It isn't always easy to find all of the ingredients.

Vegan Tacos

Level: Medium   **Serves:** 3

What you need:

- Medium sized corn tortillas
- ½ cup of raw cashews (soaked 4 hrs)
- ½ cup of black beans (soaked 6hrs)
- ½ cup of chopped avocado
- ½ cup of chopped red cabbage
- ½ cup of chopped bell peppers
- 1 cup of chopped tomatoes

- 1 tablespoon of chopped onion
- 2 tablespoons of chopped cilantro
- 2 tablespoons of olive oil
- 1 lime
- Salt to taste
- Hot sauce of your choice

How to make it:

Cashew sour cream: Drain your soaked cashews and place them in blender with a bit of fresh water, the juice of half of the lime and a pinch of salt. Blend until completely smooth.

The bean Purée: Place your soaked beans in a pot with the ½ cup of chopped tomatoes, tablespoon of chopped onion, pinch of salt and 4 times the amount of water, then cook for an hour or until they are soft. Then mix in a blender with olive oil and ¼ cup of fresh water to make your puree.

The tacos: Warm your tortillas and serve your puree with sour cream along with the rest of your ingredients on small plates. Accompany with lemon wedges and hot sauce.

Tip: If you do not have time to cook the beans, you can buy them at the supermarket already cooked in a box. Make sure they are organic and unsalted.

Eggplant Parmigiana

Level: Medium   **Serves:** 2-3

This gluten-free version will leave you drooling. It takes a bit of time and effort to make, but it is so worth it. Great for the holidays!

What you need:

- 2 big eggplants
- 4 cups of chopped and peeled tomatoes
- ½ cup of buffalo mozzarella
- 1/3 cup of grated parmigiano cheese
- 2 tablespoons of unsalted butter

- 1 teaspoon of honey
- 4 tablespoons of olive oil
- 1/3 cup of basil leaves
- 2 garlic cloves
- A pinch of red pepper flakes (optional)

How to make it:

Cut the tops and bottoms off of your eggplants and slice into ¼ inch loaves. Place on a baking tray greased with olive oil and bake for 25-30 minutes at 350-Fahrenheit degrees; then take out to cool. In the meantime, place the tomatoes and garlic in a wok/deep pan and cook over medium heat with the butter and honey for 25 minutes (the sauce will start reducing then). Add your pepper flakes and olive oil and cook for another 20 minutes until the sauce becomes a paste.

Then in a baking dish, place one layer of baked eggplant, add tomato sauce, a bit of basil leaves and some mozzarella. Make a second layer exactly the same way as the first, then add another last layer but this time without mozzarella, and sprinkled instead with parmigiano. Place in the oven for 10-15 minutes until you see the parmigiano goldening and then serve.

Tip: You can freeze your left over parmigiana by splitting into portions. You can place the frozen pieces in the oven and bake for 15 minutes. Eggplant parmigiana goes lovely with a green salad and toasted gluten-free bread.

Lemon & Thyme Sea Bream

Level: Easy   Serves: 1-2

What you need:

- A whole sea bream (dorade)
- A bunch of fresh thyme
- A lemon
- 1 garlic clove
- Olive oil
- Salt and black pepper to taste

How to make it: Rub your fish with olive oil and a little salt then place on a baking tray. In the opening of the fish's abdominal cavity, insert the garlic clove and thyme; then slice half of the lemon and place the slices on top of the fish. Bake your sea bream at 350-Fahrenheit degrees for 10-15 minutes (depending on the size). You can check if your fish is ready by opening the skin with a fork and moving the flesh. If it is cooked you should be able to move it easily, if not, place in the oven for another 2 minutes, then check again. When your fish is cooked, you can fillet it and serve with fresh olive oil, pepper and a lemon wedge.

Tip: Pair your sea bream with any of the appetizers, sides or risottos on this book. You can also use a Mediterranean see bass (branzino) for this recipe. You can see the video on how to debone and fillet a cooked fish in my youtube channel (Cooking with Adriana Londono).

Chilean Sea Bass in Chimichurri Sauce

Level: Easy   Serves: 2

What you need:

- 2 Chilean sea bass fillets
- ¼ cup parsley
- 2 tablespoons of olive oil
- 1/3 teaspoon of fresh garlic
- Salt and black pepper to taste

How to make it:

Place your fillets (rubbed with olive oil) on a baking tray and bake at 350-Fahrenheit degrees for 10 minutes. Meanwhile, blend the parsley, garlic, the olive oil, salt and pepper to taste to create your chimichurri. Make sure your fillet is cooked by cutting off a little piece of the fish (it should be tender). If not cooked all the way, place back in the oven for 2 minutes or until it is cooked (this depends on the size of the fillets). Serve your fillets topped with your chimichurri sauce.

Tip: You can use cod or halibut for this recipe. Pair your fish with any of the appetizers, sides or risottos on this book.

Mustard Salmon

Level: Easy   Serves: 2

What you need:

- 2 salmon fillets
- 3 tablespoons of olive oil
- 3 tablespoons of Dijon mustard
- Black pepper to taste

How to make it: In a pan, add 1 tablespoon of olive oil and sear your salmon fillets in medium heat. After 3 minutes, flip and cook on the other sides for a few more minutes. Cut a piece of your salmon to see if it is cooked to your taste (many people like it medium-rare; I usually cook it well). In a separate pan, warm the other 2 tablespoons of olive oil with the mustard for 30 seconds and spread on top of your seared salmon fillets; then serve.

Tip: You can use any type of mustard for this dish or trout instead of salmon. Pair your fish with any of the appetizers, sides, risottos or the lentil salad on this book.

Shrimp Saganaki

Level: Easy-medium   Serves: 2

I got this absolutely delicious recipe from a taxi driver in Athens! It can be served as an appetizer or main course.

What you need:

- 1 cup of peeled shrimp
- 1.5 cups of peeled and chopped tomatoes
- 2 tablespoons of Metaxa (optional)
- 1 tablespoon of minced onion or shallot
- 1 tablespoon of chopped parsley
- 1 tablespoon of chopped oregano
- ½ cup of sheep feta cheese
- Black or red pepper to taste

How to make it: In a deep pan or wok, place your tomatoes and onions and cook for 10 minutes at medium heat to create a sauce. Then add the Metaxa, oregano and parsley and cook for another 5. Put your shrimp in a baking pot with your freshly made tomato sauce and top with crumbled feta cheese. Bake for 10 minutes at 350-Fahrenheit degrees and serve.

Tip: Metaxa is a Greek liquor that gives this recipe a very nice taste but it isn't absolutely necessary. You can use white wine as a replacement or nothing at all.

Scallops in Pesto Sauce

Level: Easy   Serves: 1-2

What you need:

- Sea scallops (whole, choose amount to your needs)
- ½ cup of basil
- 3 tablespoons of olive oil
- 1 tablespoon of pine nuts
- ¼ teaspoon of fresh garlic
- Salt and black pepper to taste

How to make it: Pan sear the scallops for 8-10 minutes (depending on the size) with one tablespoon of olive oil. In the meantime blend your basil, pine nuts, garlic and remaining 2 tablespoons of olive oi. If too thick, add a teaspoon of water. Serve your scallops with your pesto sauce. Decorate with pine nuts if you'd like.

Tip: You can also use the chimichurri sauce from the Chilean sea bass recipe (page 119).

Avocado Key Lime Pie

Level: Easy **Serves:** 4

What you need:

- 3 medium sized avocados
- ¼ cup of fresh squeezed lime juice
- ¼ cup of honey
- 1 tablespoon coconut oil
- The zest of a lime (you can do this a carrot grater)
- ¼ cup shredded unsweetened coconut
- ½ cup dates (you have to take out their seeds)
- ½ cup pecans
- A pinch of Himalayan pink salt

How to make it: Mix the shredded coconut, pecans, dates, lime juice and salt in a food processor until you get an even paste. Then split the paste evenly between the dessert plates you are making your pies in and press it to make an even crust.

Blend the avocados, lime juice, honey, coconut oil and lime zest until creamy. Then add it evenly on top of your crusts. Decorate with a thin slice of lime and refrigerate for at least 30 minutes before eating.

Tip: You can freeze your left over pies and then eat them after thawing for 20 minutes.

Cashew Chocolate Mousse

Level: Easy   **Serves:** 2

What you need:

- 1 cup of soaked cashews (4 hours)
- ½ cup of fresh water
- 2 tablespoons of raw cacao powder
- 1 ½ tablespoons of honey or maple syrup
- 1 tablespoon of coconut oil
- 1 teaspoon of vanilla extract
- A pinch of Himalayan pink salt

How to make it: Drain the cashews and blend with the rest of the ingredients until you get a very smooth consistency. Serve with berries of your choice.

Tip: Add more water or honey if needed.

Frozen Bananas

Level: Easy   **Serves:** 4

What you need:

- 2 bananas
- 4 ice pop sticks or skewer sticks
- 3 dark chocolate bars
- 1 tablespoon of coconut oil
- 1/2 cup of chopped walnuts
- 1 mason jar
- 1 sheet of baking paper

How to make it: Peel and cut your bananas in half. Then insert them with the sticks and freeze on a plate for a couple of hours.

When your bananas are frozen, break the chocolate bars into small squares and place inside the mason jar. Then put the jar inside a pot with water and heat on the stove until the chocolate is melted. Then add the coconut oil and stir. Dip your bananas inside the jar and then sprinkle with chopped walnuts. One by one, place them on a plate covered with baking paper so that the chocolate doesn't stick to the plate. Place back in the freezer for 10 more minutes and then they'll be ready to eat.

Tip: You can use silvered almonds, chopped cashews or pecans instead of walnuts.

Ginger Root with Honey and Lemon

Level: Easy

Serves: 2

What you need:

- 2 tablespoon of chopped ginger
- 2 tablespoon of fresh lemon juice
- 2 tablespoon of honey (or to taste)
- 2 cups of water

How to make it:

Place all ingredients into a pot and cook until they boil, then serve!

Tip: Add Echinacea drops for an immune booster bomb!

Mint and Berries

Level: Easy

Serves: 2

What you need:

- ½ cup of berries of your choice
- Fresh mint (about 2 tablespoons)
- 2 tablespoons of honey
- 2 cups of water

How to make it:

In a pan, cook the berries with the honey and 2 tablespoons of water for 3 minutes. Boil the rest of your water and serve with the cooked berries and fresh mint.

Basil Pineapple

Level: Easy

Serves: 2

What you need:

- ½ cup of chopped pineapple
- Basil leaves (about 2 tablespoons)
- 2 tablespoons of honey
- 2 cups of water

How to make it:

In a pan cook the pineapple with the honey and 2 tablespoons of water for 3 minutes. Boil the rest of your water and serve with the cooked pineapple and fresh basil leaves.

Agua de Panela

Level: Easy

Serves: 2

This is a typical Colombian drink that my grandmother loves to make. It can be drank hot or cold.

What you need:

- A piece of panela (equaling 2 tablespoons)
- 2 cups of water
- ½ an apple in slices
- 2 tablespoons of fresh lime juice
- Cinnamon sticks

How to make it:
In a pot, add all the ingredients until the water boils, then serve.

Tip: Panela is raw cane sugar that comes in a block. You can find it in any Latin store/bodega.

My Story

My not-so-romantic affair with Meniere's began one morning while I was traveling by subway to work in Manhattan. All of a sudden, I felt nauseated and dizzy which forced me to get off two stops early. I knew something was wrong because I had never felt that sensation before, so I dragged myself back onto the subway and got off directly at my physician's stop. Doctor Acquista held a pen in front of my face and asked me to follow it with my gaze while he moved it from left to right making me feel even dizzier. He immediately said, "Dear Adriana, you have vertigo!" Ugh?! Vertigo?! I had only heard of the word vertigo from that Hitchcock movie and a song by U2. I then asked him what could be done about it and how long should I expect to feel that way. He said the vertigo would take about a month to subside, wrote me a prescription for Antivert, a motion sickness medicine, and sent me on my way. He was very accurate in his prognosis of the vertigo lasting about a month. It eventually faded and I went on with my life for three months until I started experiencing the vertigo again. Fun... So, I went back to Dr. Acquista who referred me to a neurologist, an ENT (ear/nose/throat specialist) and an allergist. He also ordered an MRI (magnetic resonance imagining) of my brain to discard the possibility of having a tumor. Oh Lord... That was a terrifying thought, but even scarier was getting inside the tube-shaped MRI machine, which brought on the worst panic attack.

The neurologist was convinced I had Benign Paroxysmal Positional Vertigo (BPPV), which occurs when a small piece of bone-like calcium breaks free and floats inside the inner ear canal sending confusing messages to the brain about the body's position. He had me perform these excruciating maneuvers at his office in order to aid the calcium pieces to pass through the inner canal. He would make me lie briskly on my back with my head turned towards the affected ear at a 45-degree angle while keeping it in this position for 60 seconds. He then turned my head briskly to the other side and kept it in that position for another 60 seconds. Finally, he had me roll quickly in the same direction onto my side, carrying my head along so that it was pointed nose down at a 45-degree angle for another 30 seconds. Imagine my joy...not only was I super dizzy, but he was making me feel even worse! He then prescribed vestibular rehab, which was pure torture. I had to go to his office three times a week and stare at a point on the wall while quickly moving my head from side to side and up and down. Oh lá lá! I was so aggravated with the neurologist because I was not improving with his techniques that I decided to never go back his office again. In the meantime, the ENT specialist ordered a hearing test and an excruciating caloric test, during which a technician blew hot and cold air into my ears while he read the movement of my eyes. From these tests the doctor established that I had an abnormality in my left ear causing me to have tinnitus (noise and ringing in the ear), loss of equilibrium, noise sensitivity and migraines. It was extremely frustrating that even after all of these tests, the ENT could not diagnose me. He even prescribed me steroids for a trip to India I had planned for that New Year's; however, they did absolutely nothing and I struggled during my entire trip.

Finally, I went to the last specialist I was referred to, an allergist who tested me for common allergens, but not gluten. He concluded that I was not allergic to anything and dismissed me. I also saw an acupuncturist for two months who recommended ginkgo biloba, a supplement which helps the blood flow to the brain, but I experienced no positive results. At that point when nobody could diagnose me and my life was sort of over (at least in my head), I turned to the internet. Thank goodness for the internet! With my test results in hand, I looked for causes of vertigo and one thing I had not noticed in my original research when I first started having symptoms was Meniere's disease. Meniere's was described as sudden vertigo attacks that caused people to lose their balance and drop to the ground; occurring mostly to individuals between the ages of 40 and 60. At the time, I had just turned 28 and instead of sudden vertigo attacks, I had constant dizziness. Even when I slept, I felt as if I were on a rocking boat. I also had severe fatigue, brain fog and anxiety and was becoming depressed; but since any other possibility was discarded, I looked deeper into Meniere's disease. Therefore, with my pile of test results and doctor's notes in hand, I went to see an inner ear specialist that I had researched online. He had an impressive resume and was one of the best inner ear specialists in the country as the head of the otology, neurotology and skull base surgery department at Weill Cornell Medical Center in New York City.

I sat in Dr. Selesnick's examination room while he looked through my one-year-long pile of results. He then asked me if I had ever heard of Meniere's disease, to which I replied that I had read about it online. Then, in a very calm and affirming voice he said, "You have it." I had a strong feeling that I had Meniere's, but hearing it from him was still devastating. As you may know, this illness causes hearing loss and no one wants to learn that they could lose their precious hearing, even if it is just in one ear. I had also read online that there was no cure for the disease, but some risky surgeries were being performed to relieve the symptoms. I was so desperate that I begged him to operate on my affected ear, but he was hesitant as I was young and I could risk losing my hearing completely in that ear and/or have facial paralysis. He then prescribed me a diuretic to lower the sodium in my body, told me to reduce my salt intake to no more than 1500mg per day, to not smoke and to stop drinking caffeine. What?! Smoking I could live without since I had always been a social smoker, but salt and caffeine?? I pretty much put salt on everything! Oranges, apples, avocados…green mango with lime juice and salt? My favorite snack! At this time in my life I was also having 5 espressos a day since I was working in real estate in New York City for two crazy bosses from Italy, and I needed all the caffeine I could get.

Following my doctor's recommendations I gave up caffeine which was, for a Colombian girl who started drinking coffee at age 5, one of the most difficult things I have ever done. Café con leche was a staple in my family's breakfast and "tinto" (a small cup of black coffee), was the norm in the mid-afternoon. I brought my salt intake down significantly as well and I took my medicine as directed. Also, after my diagnosis in the effort to try to be as healthy as possible, I started following the Mediterranean Prescription which is a book written by my physician, Doctor Acquista. It got me started on a healthy diet that included lots of vegetables, fruits and legumes, decreased red meat/dairy intake, and also included eating a good amount of fatty fish. By doing all of these things, I finally started feeling better or semi-normal. I experienced some dizziness at times and occasional fatigue in the afternoons, which would force me to take a nap on my desk or on the couch of the apartments I happened to be showing that afternoon. Thankfully, the naps really helped as I had more energy afterwards and because espresso was now off the table, this was my only way of coping with the tiredness. At that time I also started cooking more for myself because I would not trust any restaurant with salt. In fact, I was pretty terrified of it, as it is the first thing one is recommended to drastically reduce after diagnosis. Later, after years of coping with Meniere's and trying everything under the sun except for surgery, I realized that salt was not the enemy. The true enemy was added sodium to processed foods and table salt, but not necessarily all salts. However, thanks to my fear of salt and making all of the delicious recipes in my doctor's book, I became very good at cooking.

Since I began feeling much better and wanted to take a break from Manhattan and from work, I decided to move to Rome, dolce vita, Rome! So there I was on September of 2009 living in one of the most beautiful cities in the world and learning Italiano! While in Rome I started an online villa rental company so that I could manage my time better and cook for myself. I discovered amazing dishes while dining at restaurants and from my new Italian friends who were very happy to share their cooking techniques and secrets with me. After a year in Rome, I moved to Paris and then married a Parisian whose family owned an organic vineyard in Burgundy. The wine they produced was so good I drank it a couple of times a week without it causing any dizziness or triggering an attack. On the other hand, when I went out to a restaurant and had non-organic wine, the opposite would happen and I would have a reaction. Interesting! During my time at this lovely vineyard, I ate either organic produce that I grew myself or bought at the farmer's market in Beaune, a city close to Dijon. Also, while in France I started taking Betahistine, which is the medication prescribed in Europe for Meniere's disease. Back then my symptoms seemed to stay under control, except for in the winter months when the cold weather would trigger my dizziness. Therefore, I decided to move to Los Angeles where the sun always shines and the winters feel like spring.

Here in LA I continued to have a very strict organic diet, which was mostly plant-based. However, it was not until I went back to New York City for Thanksgiving of 2014 that I made a breakthrough discovery! While visiting my mom, I ate at restaurants most of the time and had bread, pizza, cupcakes, etc. Well, it did not take long before my old friends vertigo, fatigue and brain fog came back making me feel completely powerless. On the plane back to LA, seated next to me was a lady who took an interest in my deaf French Bulldog, Paco. She noticed I was not feeling well and asked me what was wrong. I told her I had vertigo caused by Meniere's disease and to my surprise, she knew what Meniere's was. She explained she was a holistic healer and recommended that I stop eating gluten, which to her knowledge causes inflammation in the human body. She believed my inner ear was most likely being affected by a gluten allergy or sensitivity and advised me to eat anti-inflammatory foods such as ginger and turmeric. When I got home, I immediately went online to research if there was any connection between gluten and Meniere's disease and indeed there was! There was a study done in Milan in which a total of 58 patients between ages of 35 and 66, who were diagnosed with definite Meniere's disease, were recruited. A total of 33 Meniere's disease patients (56.9%) proved to be sensitive to gliadin, 8 of whom were positive to a prick test after 20 minutes, 13 after 6 hours, 11 after 12 hours, and one after 24 hours. The gliadins are a family of glutamine- and proline- rich monomeric proteins that account for 40% to 50% of the total protein content of wheat kernels.[4] There was also a recent study done on a 62-year-old woman who was successfully treated for tinnitus, dizziness and nausea with a gluten-free diet.[5] Eliminating gluten was the one thing I had not yet tried and believe me, I loved my gluten! I have always been a fan of Italian cuisine and pasta, of course, but at that point, I said to hell with it, I would try avoiding it for a couple of months. And guess what? My symptoms went away and I was feeling better than ever! Therefore, I decided to do the unthinkable: I stopped my medicine! After 7 years of thinking I could never live without it, but knowing it was going to destroy my liver at some point and bring who knows what other side effects, I decided to stop the Betahistine and have been medicine-free ever since.

Thankfully, I was able to begin healing and I believe that I am stopping the progression of the disease with my Meniere's diet, which you can also follow. It took me a long way to get here and to understand the triggers and helpers. I hope my experiences, recipes do's and don'ts can aid you in beginning your own journey towards recovery and living a normal life. I absolutely love cooking and am utterly convinced that you are what you eat. Now that new degenerative and autoimmune diseases are showing up, I strongly believe it is something, or perhaps a combination, of things we are ingesting that are making us ill. We live in an era of processed foods, genetically modified organisms (GMOs), and an overdose of pesticides and herbicides in agricultural practices. Also, cattle and poultry are being fed antibiotics and GMO diets, and are being treated with hormones. We are being attacked from all fronts with chemicals, neurotoxins, poisons and hormones. No wonder we are getting sick! In order to take back control of your life and manage your Meniere's, I recommend you start with your diet. Remember that your body is your temple and foundation. If you lead a healthy life and take control of everything you ingest, not only will your Meniere's symptoms improve significantly but you will also be preventing other diseases from developing in your body. And let's be honest, who has the time and energy to dedicate to another disease? I surely do not! I already have my hands full with Meniere's!

Bibliography

1. Gold, Mark. "Docket # 02P-0317 Recall Aspartame as a Neurotoxic Drug: File #4: Reported Aspartame Toxicity Reactions." Message to FDA Dockets Submittal. 12 Jan. 2003. E-mail.

2. Peretz, Jackye, et al. "Bisphenol A and Reproductive Health: Update of Experimental and Human Evidence, 2007–2013." Environmental Health Perspectives. 122.8 (2014): n.p. Web. 27 Aug. 2015.

3. "GMO Facts." NonGMOProject. Non-GMO Project, n.d. Web. 27 Aug. 2015.

4. Barozzi, Stefania, Luca Del Bo, and Antonio Cesarani. "The effect of a gluten-free diet on a Person with severe tinnitus." International Tinnitus Journal. 18.2 (2013): 134-37. Web. 27 Aug. 2015.

5. Di Berardino, Federica and Antonio Cesarani. "Gluten Sensitivity in Meniere's Disease." 122.3 (2012):700-02. Web. 27 Aug. 2015.

Contact

Website: www.menierescookbook.com (visit my website for latest news and research on Meniere's disease, sample menus and videos)

Facebook: www.facebook.com/menierescookbook (like Meniere's Cookbook)

Youtube Channel: Cooking with Adriana Londono (check out my latest videos of recipes and cooking/grocery shopping tips)

Instagram: cookingwithadriana (follow me on my culinary adventures)

Credits

Design:

Stephen Hutchison

Photography:

Stephen Hutchison
Rafael Leyva
Kiko Kairuz

Editing:

Soraya Finley Londono
Sarah Crenshaw

Adriana Londono Ventures, INC.

25635972R20080

Made in the USA
San Bernardino, CA
07 November 2015